D1321251

A BOOK OF FRIENDSHIP AND FLOWERS

*A pictorial selection of flowers
and gardens throughout the year
with verses by*
Kathleen Partridge

Jarrold Colour Publications

The delicate white Snowdrop on its slender stem, and the cheerful golden Aconite with its shiny leaves are among the first to show their flowers in the New Year, and bloom from January to March.

The Snowdrop *means Hope*; the Aconite—*Misanthropy*

THE MESSAGE

When petals fall the flowers speak
With every bouquet spent.
They speak of love and friendship
Through the subtlety of scent.

Of hope and peace and happiness
Of courage, joy or fear
Each petal sends a message
To the one who cares to hear.

And those who love and those who part
And those who only wait
Will find their message woven
In the tapestry of Fate.

Crocus *means Youthful Gladness*; Saffron Crocus—*Mirth*

THE COMING OF FRIENDS

We long for you and look for you
In wintry winds and rain
Waiting for your visit
To make us young again.

Forsythia, grape hyacinths
And hawthorn down the dell
All of them will blossom
In time to wish you well.

Catkins in the copses
And violets in the hollow
Carpeting the footpaths
For friendly feet to follow.

The Crocus (*left*) has funnel-shaped flowers of yellow, purple or white, which appear in the spring or autumn. *Above:* An arrangement of Narcissi, Anemones and Muscari.

Daffodils *mean Regard*; the Giant Yellow *are for Chivalry*

COME OUT TO PLAY

When the air vibrates with springtime
Budding leaves replace the old
And hearts grow light with promise
As the earth spills out her gold.

And so arrive the daffodils
In glorious array
To call us and enthrall us
And to take our breath away.

Wild Daffodils at Farndale, North Yorkshire

The graceful white Narcissus (*above*) is native to central and Mediterranean Europe and parts of the Far East. In this country it flowers between March and May. The Speedwell (*right*) has small blue flowers consisting of four lobes, and its leaves are paired. It flowers between March and August and is pollinated by hover-flies.

Narcissus *means Egotism*; Speedwell—*Fidelity*

FAITHFUL TO THE SPRING

Lord who made the fields and flowers
And set the sky with stars alight.
Who rinsed the earth in dew and showers
To wash the narcis extra white.

Lord who brought a world of wonder
And set the silver in the blue
Break the hardened soil asunder
To bring the speedwell shining through.

Orchids *mean A Belle*; Scillas—*Forgive and Forget*

BE HAPPY FRIEND

The flowers that springtime promised
Have bloomed in winter's wake
Old troubles grow less wearisome
And hearts forget to ache.

Maybe love lies bleeding
But the flax will never fail
And orchids are a miracle
That make the sun turn pale.

The scilla bells are ringing
With the sweetest music yet
Calling all who listen
To forgive and to forget.

There are over 15,000 varieties of Orchid (*left*), mostly from the tropics. In Britain these gorgeous, elaborate flowers are usually cultivated in special greenhouses, although a few can be grown in the garden. The bell-shaped flowers of the Spanish Squill (*above*) may be pink, blue or white, and grow in slender racemes on eighteen-inch-long stems. They are shown here with the handsome foliage of the Hosta (or Plantain Lily).

Primroses *mean Evrly Youth*; Polyanthus—*Confidence*

POSTE HASTE

Primroses and periwinkles
Violets and views
Palm and polyanthus
In the daily news.

Youngest of the springtime
Open faces, starry eyes
Turning to the world
A look of permanent surprise.

The young at heart will gather
And arrange them in a bowl
Because they treasure secrets
But they never tell a soul.

The Primrose (*left*) is a favourite English wild flower, and its narrow crinkly leaves and pale yellow flowers are to be found nestling in hedgerows and woods between March and May. The Polyanthus (*below*) is of garden origin and bears its flowers in clusters on erect stems. The flowers are of various colours, but each has a yellow centre.

The Pasque Flower (*above*) flowers between April and May. These flowers may be mauve, violet, purple or red, with golden anthers, and they have silky outsides. The leaves are hairy and finely divided. The Saxifrage (*right*) is a small, shell-pink, rock-garden flower, which grows to about four inches in height, and flowers between February and April. The small, rounded, sky-blue flowers of the Muscari (*right*) are clustered on stems up to nine inches in height and flower in April and May.

Pasque Flower *means* 'You have no claims';
Saxifrage—*Affection*

EVERYDAY FRIENDS

Saxifrage called London Pride
An easy growing one
Contented in the shade
As it is happy in the sun.

When mixed with high or humble blooms
As neighbourly and nice
Growing in abnndance
And never thinking twice.

Like kindly friends and neighbours
Always near to bear the brunt
As happy in the back row
As they would be in the front.

FAIRY FLOWERS

Perfect are the petals on a palette leaf of green.
Poised like fairy wings embroidered for the Fairy
Queen. These cyclamens called 'diffident' are shy,
but not forlorn. Shiny as the sunset and as delicate
as dawn.

Isn't it amazing how the petals are uncurled.
To think that we awake to find such beauty in the
world!

There are many species of Cyclamen (*left*). The flowers may be white, pink, deep rose, mauve or purple, and the flowering season varies according to species. The foliage has attractive markings. The Erythronium or Trout Lily (*above*) has delicate pink drooping heads with orange anthers. They hang from slender stems which are about ten inches in height.

Tulip (Yellow) *means Hopeless Love*; Red—*Declaration of Love*

STRENGTH FOR THE DAY

A gift of tulips is a loving token
A feeling of affection never spoken
So long to last, so sturdy to behold
In pink or purple, multi-toned or gold.

Though massed by millions in the tulip fields
A few set in a vase much pleasure yields
So will affection blossom in the room
With strength for the day in every upright bloom.

Pieris forrestrii (*above*) has clusters of tiny white flowers and bright red foliage on the young shoots. *Right:* Double pink Tulips with golden stamens.

Tulip (White) *means 'Forget me not'*
but Forget Me Not *means 'True Love'*

REMEMBER ME

Gracious garden tended
By the love of many hands
Years of thought have blended
Where the weeping willow stands.

The old house gazes downwards
From her windows near the sky
And hopes the world remembers her
When time has passed her by.

There's virtue in the soil
That has been turned by countless spades
And in earth's heart a seed is dropped
By every flower that fades.

There are many varieties of garden Tulips and also a great range of colours. According to the variety, they flower between April and June. The lovely little blue flowers of the Forget-Me-Not also bloom in the spring.

The familiar Bluebell (*above*) of the English woods blooms between April and June. Also to be found in the woods at that time of the year is the Three-angled Garlic (*right*), which has three-cornered stems and large white flowers.

Bluebells *mean Constancy*; Birch—*Meekness*

CARPET OF BLUE

Bluer than a sailor's eyes
Bluer than the bluest skies
Spread your carpet, ring your bells
Round the trees and down the dells.

Call a meeting place for friends
In the woods where anger ends.
Tell two hearts for Truelove's sake
To keep the loving vows they make.

Though trains may whistle, traffic roar
And aircraft in the heavens soar
Though houses rise and cities fall
The bluebells grow in spite of all.

Azaleas (Japanese) *mean Temperance*; Indian—*True to the End*

FLOWERS FROM THE EAST

In far off lands discoveries
Were made by Pioneers
Strange plants, strange foods, strange animals
Were brought home through the years.

Azaleas were also brought
From India and Japan
And all this loveliness
Grows from the forethought of one man.

There are many species of Azalea and they come mostly from India and the Far East. However, they grow well in England and are gay with colour in the spring.

Dicentra spectabilis or Bleeding Heart (*below*) has deep rose, heart-shaped flowers hanging from arching stems, and it flowers in the spring. The Lily-of-the-Valley (*right*) has tiny, white, fragrant, bell-shaped flowers on short stalks, which bloom in May and June. The Musk (*right*) has yellow flowers spotted with red and blooms in June and July.

Dicentra (*Bleeding Heart*); Lily of the Valley—
Return of Happiness; Musk—*unconscious sweetness*

BE HAPPY NOW

Unaware the little Lily
Of our love and our affection
She snuggles in the shadow of a leaf
For her protection.

Too shy to ring her bell
And boast the beauty of her birth
Yet the perfume of her petals
Is the sweetest scent on earth.

No wonder that the hearts will bleed
That overhang her shelter
And the musk will cuddle closer
In the hope that he may melt her.

The *Paeonia suffruticosa* (*above*) is the Moutan Tree Paeony which grows to about five feet tall with rose-coloured flowers. It blooms in May and June. The Lupin (*right*) from North America carries its flowers on long spikes, three to four feet high. There is a great range of colours, and the flowering season is in June.

Paeonia (paeony) *means bashfulness*; Lupin—*Voraciousness*

LONERS

Big and bright and beautiful
The other flowers they shun
Unlike the genial lupin
Who is friends with everyone.

Like to the hardy people
Who are purposeful and proud
Who bloom in sunny solitude
Yet wither in a crowd.

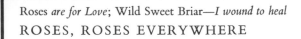

Roses *are for Love*; Wild Sweet Briar—*I wound to heal*

ROSES, ROSES EVERYWHERE

In the heart of every rose
A pearl of dew prepares to settle
Eternal summer lingers
In the texture of a petal.

A rose will grace a mansion
Her intrusion needs no pardon
She is equally at home
In any little cottage garden.

The rose garden, Stanton Harcourt Manor, Oxfordshire

There are many varieties of Rose (*above*), and these provide a
mass of colour and fragrance from June until autumn. *Right:*
Red Roses and white Daisies.

Daisy *means Innocence*; Deep Red Rose—*I blush for shame*

FLOWERS FOR A CHILD

Daisy white you look so pert
In your spotless frilly skirt.
Innocent, and yet I wist
By the crimson roses kissed.

Daisy pied and starry eyed
Carmine lips to you are plied
All the children know your name
Yet the roses blush for shame.

Growing winsome, growing wild
Just the keepsake for a child
Whose joy and laughter you must share
To make a daisy chain to wear.

Pyrethrums *mean 'I am not changed, they wrong me'*; Dimorphotheca
—*Star of the Veldt*

JOURNEY WITH JOY

Such a ponderous name for a beautiful flower
That shines in the dark at the midnight hour.
On African nights in the heat and the dust
When there's no one to turn to and no one to trust.

A flower of such beauty it hardly seems real
Of perfect proportion and special appeal
The star of the Veldt, making travellers aware
That God guards us all from His Heaven up there.

Pyrethrums, more simple, but sturdier yet
Are a flower that we pluck and as quickly forget.
So like any daisy, a friend for the day
Sent to bless us, caress us, and lighten our way.

Pyrethrums (*left*) come from Persia and the Caucasus. There are various shades, and they flower in June. The strikingly beautiful flowers of the *Dimorphotheca 'Jucunda'* (*above*) has South African origins and blooms between June and September.

Honeysuckle *means Devoted Affection*; Sweet Pea—*Delicate Pleasure*

OLD FASHIONED FLOWERS

It's the old fashioned honeysuckle
The common hedgerow kind
That has the sweetest smell
And leaves a memory behind.

It's the old fashioned sweet peas
Like baby butterflies
That fill the room with fragrance
And entrance our waking eyes.

The fragrant Honeysuckle (*left*) is common in woods and hedgerows, and there are also garden varieties. The delicate flowers appear in the summer. The dainty Sweet Pea (*below*), which comes from southern Europe, climbs by means of tendrils and grows from six to ten feet. The delicately scented flowers grow two or more to a stem and in a great many shades, and appear from midsummer onwards.

There are hundreds of garden varieties of Iris (*above*). Amidst sword-like foliage the flowers are borne on two- to four-foot stems. They usually bloom between May and June and there are various shades, usually netted or veined with another shade or colour. The Erigeron (*right*) has mauve, daisy-like flowers with orange centres that are not unlike Michaelmas Daisies. They flower between June and October.

Iris *means A Message*; Erigeron (Fleabane)—*North American Daisy*

SHADES OF PURPLE

Colour of an autumn sky
Where pink and purple clouds race by
Bringing happy thoughts to those
Who make the most of summer's close.

Likewise the iris, set in green
Royal purple as a queen
'Raise your head and smile and wave'
Is that the way we should behave?

Waterlilies on a lake
What a restful sight they make!
Flat the leaves that quiver slightly
Where the wagtails tread so lightly.

Hawks and herons come and go
Where the peaceful waters flow
When foxgloves toll for time and tide
The lilies close at eventide.

The Waterlily (*above*) has large starry blooms and its leaves are also large. The tall stems of the Foxglove (*right*) bear many slightly drooping tubular flowers.

Mesembryanthemums (*above*) have South African origins and thrive in dry, sun-baked soils. The daisy-like flowers, which appear in midsummer, are of brilliant shades of pink, red, white, yellow and orange and grow to about four inches tall. The succulent leaves are about three inches long. The Anemone or Windflower (*right*) has elegantly cut foliage and branching stems, bearing open white, pink, scarlet or purple flowers about two to three inches across. They flower in late summer and make good border plants.

Mesembryanthemum *means Idleness*;
Anemones—*Expectation*

NICKNAMES

The nicknames of the flowers
Must be as old as Father Time.
Pert, appealing, pretty
Set to music and to rhyme.

Thrift and Grannies Bonnet,
Rose of Sharon, Meadow Rue.
Jacob's Ladder, Creeping Jenny,
Shepherd's Needle, Bird's-eye Blue.

Who named the Thyme and Tonguebleed,
Old Man's Beard, and Dragonwort,
And set the Ragged Robin,
Next to Break your Mother's Heart?

OVER THE WALL

The clematis must climb the wall
To see the other side.
The hollyhocks are curious too
And Rosebay has a lovely view
Outgazing far and wide.
Yet none of them will beg your pardon
When they peer into your garden
Always reaching for a better view.
Such saucy flowers, although not ours.
'I'd love some in my garden. . . . Wouldn't you?'

Left: The Rosebay in its natural setting. *Above:* An arrangement
of purple Clematis flowers and orange Montbretia.

Phlox *means Unanimity*; Cedar—*Strength*

ALL FRIENDS TOGETHER

An old fashioned garden of old fashioned flowers.
Tansy and teasle on bankside and bowers.
A friendly profusion of lily and phlox
Carnations and cornflowers, verbena and stocks.

The pathways are peaceful, the moss is caressing
The scent of the lavender offers a blessing
And somewhere a sundial is telling the hours
In a friendly old garden of old fashioned flowers.

The garden, Sudeley Castle, Gloucestershire

Lilies (White) *mean Purity*; Gloxinia—*Proud Spirit*

REVERENCE

No colour is so right
To clothe the Lily as the white
Waxen as a candle
On the altar cloth at night.

To pluck it like a primrose
Would be sacrilege as such
She is too fair to fondle
And too beautiful to touch.

Crinum powellii album (*left*) is an extremely attractive hybrid flower with tropical origins. There are several flowers, each three to four inches across, on each stem. The stems grow to about fifteen inches in height. Gloxinias (*below*) are varieties of *Sinningia speciosa* and produce richly coloured velvety-like flowers from midsummer until early autumn. These are various shades of red, blue and purple and also white.

The *Amaryllis belladonna* (*above*) was introduced to English gardens from Cape Colony in 1712. The slender stems carry several scented white or pink flowers which bloom in August and September. The Passiflora or Passion Flower (*right*) is a vigorous climber, and its elaborate flowers appear from June to September.

Belladonna *means Silence*; Passion Flower—*Religious Superstition*

FROM HEAVEN TO EARTH

The sunbeams dance down from a shaft out of Heaven
The perfume soars up where the lark sweetly sings
And that's why these flowers wear celestial colours
The delicate texture of Angel's wings.

And deep in the heart of the sweet Passion Flower
The stamens are formed as the Calvary Cross
Stained by the blood of Our Lord's Crown of Thorns
Marked by the tears that were shed for His loss.

Ivy *means Fidelity*

WINTER FRIEND

Some call it 'poison Ivy'
But it is a winter friend
And stays when Red Hot Pokers fade
And Tiger Lilies end.

Constant and contented
On the garden wall it grows
Sheltering the birds
From every stormy wind that blows.

Left: Summer's Red-hot Pokers blend well with the evergreen Ivy. *Above:* The stately, purple-spotted, orange flowers of *Lilium 'Prairie Harlequin'*.

The Hydrangea, of which there are many varieties, originates from the Far East and is a favourite shrub among British gardeners. It can be grown successfully in most parts of the British Isles and is popular on account of its profuse clusters of flowers among ample foliage. The flower-clusters bloom in summer and autumn in shades of pink, blue, red or white.

Hydrangea *means Heartless Boaster*; Ferns *are for Fascination*

MELLOW MOMENTS

Ferns for Fascination
When the world is green and wild
Shelter for the little creatures
Cover for a child.

And when hydrangeas lose their hue
With petals paper thin
We know that summer's going out
And winter coming in.

Above: The orange and red flowers of the Nasturtium make a gay summer show. *Right:* In spring, summer and winter there are varieties of Pansy blooming to gladden the heart.

Pansies *are for thoughts*; Nasturtiums—*Patriotism*

'HEARTSEASE'

Pansy, prettiest of flowers
Open faced to sun and showers
Velvet as the backs of bees
Call them 'heartsease' if you please

And the spur of the nasturtium
Takes the bees on an excursion
Deep down in the pointed tip
We can taste it if we sip.

Grown with joy in sunny places
With every colour in their faces
Gather them before they wane
And they will quickly grow again.

Begonia *means Dark Thoughts*; Yew—*Sorrow*

EVERGREEN

The yew is for sorrow, but green is the leaf
Keeping its foliage even in grief.
That is the reason why yews go not bare
But point to new hope in the midst of old care.

And evergreen colours are not born to die
But decorate earth when the summer goes by
They cover the landscape while earth takes a rest
Immortal, heartlifting, and by our Lord blessed.

Massed begonias in the Topiary Garden, Levens Hall

Dahlia *means Instability*

LAST TO REIGN

The Queen of all the garden there she stands
While Autumn tints the world with golden hands.
Reigning alone, the dahlia rules the world
With buttons, pompons or with spikes uncurled.

And there are some that rule as if in state
With blossoms like a giant golden plate.
And those with ragged curls that sweetly swing
As if to give the earth her final fling.

The Dahlia (*above*) is a decorative flower from Mexico and
Guatemala, and there are many varieties. *Right:* Orange
Chinese Lanterns with the berries of the Berberis.

Above: An autumnal arrangement of Bulrushes and colourful Chrysanthemums. *Right:* The Poinsettia is a showy, easy, long-living plant.

Chrysanthemums (Yellow) *mean Slighted Love*; Bullrushes—*Docility*

BROKEN HEARTED

I bid you love remember
When you are fancy free
That not so very long ago
You were attached to me.

Chrysanthemums you sent me
Gold as the sun above
Knowing that the meaning of these flowers
Was 'Slighted Love'.

So press this petal in a book
And on some distant day
You'll open it to take a look
And steal my heart away.

Christmas Rose *means Relieve My Anxiety*

THE FAIREST FLOWER

The leaves are green as friendship
That lasts the winter through.
The blossoms shine on darker days
As dear friends always do.

Peace, to the heart that grieves you bring
And joy to the anxious mind.
O lovely Christmas Rose
Just for a friend you are designed.

The delightful Christmas Rose (*above*) has large white flowers
with yellow anthers, and blooms in the winter months.

Published and Printed in Great Britain by Jarrold & Sons Ltd, Norwich
85306 400 8 © Jarrold & Sons Ltd, Norwich 380